PUNCTUATION

RULES and PRACTICE 1

Susan J. Daughtrey M.Ed.

Childs World Education Limited
1995

CONTENTS

THE IMPORTANCE OF CORRECT PUNCTUATION

Correct punctuation is essential if we are going to avoid ambiguity and convey, in writing, precise meaning. Look at this sentence:

Michael said Pat is ill today.

You have probably already decided who said what about whom. But are you correct? *Who*, exactly is ill?
Is Michael *reporting* that Pat is ill?

Michael said Pat is ill today.

Is Michael actually *saying* that Pat is ill?

Michael said, "Pat is ill today."

or is Pat telling us Michael is ill?

"Michael," said Pat, "is ill today."

We can see from this example, that without correct punctuation the sentence is ambiguous and unclear making it difficult for the reader to understand. When this happens the reader is likely to lose confidence in the author and the author's words will lose their effect.

What exactly is the situation here?

My brother is a famous acrobat as well as a juggler he can juggle six balls at once he is really skilled on Tuesday he is going to appear on T.V.

What a show that will be! An acrobat juggling six balls and a juggler!
Can he do the same, one wonders, on Thursdays and Saturdays?
Or have I got it wrong? Perhaps it should be:

My brother is a famous acrobat as well as a juggler. He can juggle six balls at once. He is really skilled. On Tuesday he is going to appear on T.V.

Barry drives a truck while parked alongside the road one day he saw two deer jumping down from his cab with a sandwich in one hand and a camera in the other he took a whole roll of film they were magnificent photographs. Everyone in the family is talking about them.

I bet! I shouldn't think it is every day you see a deer-photographer eating sandwiches in a truck! Or have I got it wrong? Should it be:

Barry drives a truck. While parked alongside the road one day, he saw two deer. Jumping down from his cab, with a sandwich in one hand and a camera in the other, he took a whole roll of film. They were magnificent photographs. Everyone in the family is talking about them.

The purpose of proper punctuation then, is to help to make the meaning of what you write clearer for the reader, and to prevent ambiguity.

There are 12 punctuation topics which we shall look at:
1. Capital letters.
2. Final Punctuation Marks: the Full Stop, Exclamation Mark and Question Mark.
3. Commas.
4. Direct and Reported speech.
5. The Semi-colon.
6. The Colon.
7. Brackets.
8. The Dash.
9. The Hyphen.
10. Inverted Commas.
11. Quotation Marks.
12. The Apostrophe.

These two books of *Punctuation Rules and Practice* will look at each punctuation mark in detail. The Rules of Punctuation will be discussed and summarised, and Practice Exercises will be given to practice each Rule, one at a time. At the back of this book and *Punctuation Rules and Practice 2*, Rule Summaries will be given for you to complete and copy onto cards thus creating your own set of revision cards for future reference.

Let us begin by looking at a sentence, what is meant by it and its structure and punctuation.

THE SENTENCE

What is a sentence?

A *sentence* is a sequence of words which:
    1. Tries to articulate a complete and unified idea.
    2. Makes complete sense by itself, and as such,
    3. Can stand alone.
It needs no other words to complete it.

If you went up to someone and said *up the hill, I was in the park when, the sun shone round, what's the difference between?* that person would wonder what you were talking about (and would probably wait for you to add more words to complete the meaning). These words are meaningless. Such groups of words make no sense and cannot stand alone. They are not sentences. If however, you were to say,

The wind is blowing in the trees

this does make complete sense, does convey meaning, can stand alone and is therefore a sentence.

PRACTICE : THE SENTENCE

What is a sentence?

A Sentence is a sequence of words which:
   1. Tries to articulate a complete and unified idea.
   2. Makes complete sense by itself, and as such,
   3. Can stand alone.
It needs no other words to complete it.

Exercise One:

Some of the following groups of words are sentences (because they make complete sense and can stand alone), others are not. Copy out the complete sentences *only*, adding a capital letter and a full stop.

1. the cat on the mat

2. the sun shone brightly

3. reading the newspaper

4. in the basket

5. she went shopping

6. under the bed

7. do your homework

8. that exercise is silly

9. on the windowsill

10. i like to travel by car

Exercise Two:

Copy out and correctly punctuate the groups of words below *which are complete sentences*.

1. in the middle of the lounge carpet

2. i have a kitten called harry

3. draw the curtains

4. i have never seen

5.   he opened his eyes

6.   in the book on the desk

7.   walking down the street

8.   john will have a piece of chocolate

9.   you need a new pair of shoes

10. in the wardrobe on a hanger

Exercise Three: _____

As above, write out those groups of words below which are sentences. Don't forget to use a capital letter at the beginning of the sentence, and a full stop at the end.

1.   in the summer holidays

2.   i like swimming

3.   when the sun comes up

4.   in the kitchen drawer

5.   it is jessica's birthday

6.   you can have a new pair of trainers

7.   i can help

8.   the tyre is flat

9.   on the other side of the page

10. in the back garden

A sentence then conveys precise meaning. It is an expression of ideas; it is a group of words which makes complete sense and as such can stand alone. It needs no other words to help explain it.

The statements above are enough for *simple* sentences:

The cat sat on the mat.
The cow jumped over the moon.
Susan has brown hair.

These are all *simple* sentences, are groups of words which make complete sense by themselves and can stand alone. Each conveys precise meaning that cannot be misunderstood by the reader.

However, sometimes more than this is needed.

Writing is usually not so straightforward. We do not write in *simple* sentences all the time. Sometimes a sentence has several parts to it.
Example:
> Thomasina, the cat, was in the kitchen drinking milk while
> her new kittens were trying to get into the garden.

This is a *complex* sentence. It has several parts. We could put a full stop after *Thomasina, the cat, was in the kitchen drinking milk*. These words follow all the rules of a sentence:
> They convey precise meaning.
> They make complete sense by themselves.
> They can stand alone.

But if we were to do this we would be left with, *while her new kittens were trying to get into the garden*. These words do not make sense by themselves, cannot stand alone, and are not a sentence. The only way these words make sense is by adding them to the first group of words. Together they make a complete sentence.
So now we must revise what we mean by a sentence:
1. A sentence conveys precise meaning.
2. It is a group of words which makes complete sense.
3. As such it can stand alone. However,
4. Sometimes we must add other groups of words which cannot stand as sentences on their own.

Main and Subordinate Clauses.   For those who need more information.
The main part of the sentence which is complete and can stand alone is called the *main clause*. The parts of a sentence which cannot stand by themselves but need to be added to the main clause to make sense, are called *subordinate clauses*. A main clause can stand alone as a sentence, a subordinate clause cannot.

A *complex* sentence is made up of more than one clause. The main part or *main clause*, and one or more *subordinate clauses*. A *subordinate clause* is introduced by words such as *although, if, while* and *when* and has a specific function, or job to do, rather than having the ability to function as a separate sentence in its own right. It may do the job of a noun, an adjective, or an adverb. If a subordinate clause does the work of an adjective it is known as an *adjectival clause*, if it does the work of an adverb of time answering the question *when does the action take place?* it is an *adverbial clause* of time, and so on.
Example:
> Main clause: I shall do my homework
> Subordinate clause: when I have had my tea.

This subordinate clause is an *adverbial clause of time* - answers the question *when?*

> Complete sentence: When I have had my tea, I shall do my homework.
>   or   I shall do my homework when I have had my tea.

We place a comma after a subordinate clause if it precedes the main clause of the sentence. If the main clause comes first in the sentence, no comma is necessary. (See point 9 The Comma.)

A *compound sentence* is slightly different. It contains at least two *co-ordinating clauses* which may be joined together by a conjunction such as *and, but* or *or*. Co-ordinating clauses are of equal status. One clause does not have the function of describing, qualifying or modifying the other as a subordinate clause does with a main clause. Indeed, both clauses could stand alone as sentences in their own right.
Example:

Co-ordinating clauses: He is reading a newspaper.
                                She is writing a letter.
              He is reading a newspaper, *and* she is writing a letter.

There is usually a comma before the conjunction when the subject of each co-ordinating clause is different. (See point 11 The Comma.)
If the subject remains the same there is no need for a comma.
Example:

              He is reading a newspaper and (he is) smoking a pipe.

A *phrase* is a group of words which forms part of a clause or sentence but does not contain a finite verb (with tense and subject) and cannot stand alone and make sense.
Example:

                        ...the cat on the mat...
                        ...up the hill on the left...

Exercise Four:_____

Some of the following groups of words are one sentence only, and some are two. Rewrite each group of words adding a capital letter and a full stop where necessary.

1.   it was raining michael decided to take his umbrella

2.   sandra was tired so she decided to go to bed early

3.   come to my house to watch television

4.   i like school best on saturday

5.   my shoes need repairing they let in water

6.   in my bag there's a pen

7.   we can go to the beach take a towel

8.   the football pitch was muddy we slipped about

9.   the radio is too loud please turn it down

10. the roses are beautiful they have lasted a long time

Exercise Five: _____

Some of the following groups of words are one sentence, some two and some more. Rewrite them, correctly punctuating each one.

1.   it's raining i must go or i shall get wet

2.   the phone rang just as i was about to leave

3.   in her bag there's a book take it to her she needs it now

4.   the dog needs taking for a walk he's gone to get his lead

5.   the newspaper boy is late he was late yesterday and the day before

6.   let's go shopping i need to buy a new pair of shoes

7.   this will have to wait i'm busy making tea i haven't got the time

8.   after i've done my homework, i'm going to watch t.v.

9.   i like to play badminton i'm in the county team now

10. sara wears a funny hat she's got orange hair as well

11. christopher has an american tea shirt on it looks swell

For clarity of meaning, effectiveness and maximum reader-enjoyment, it is essential that an author is aware of the importance of correct punctuation. Punctuation is essential to good writing. The Rules of Punctuation are there to be used as the writer's tools and every writer should make it his business to know them and to know them well. Almost every part of a written piece of work has structure and conforms to certain patterns and rules. Without these patterns and rules, writing would be chaotic and the written word would become less effective and cease to convey precise and enriched meaning. Let us begin by looking at the structure of the simplest coherent unit of writing, the sentence.

THE STRUCTURE OF A SENTENCE

Every sentence has its structure defined in three terms. It must have:

1.   **A Capital letter at the beginning.**
2.   **A Final punctuation mark. And usually,**
3.   **A subject and predicate containing a finite verb.**
      (A *finite verb* can have a subject and can form a tense.)

Since this book deals specifically with the Rules of Punctuation, we shall concern ourselves only with the first two points of those above. The third point is dealt with separately in *Grammar Rules and Practice* in this Series of Books.

CAPITAL LETTERS

Every sentence must begin with a capital letter.

There are 9 other uses of the capital letter:
1. **The pronoun *I*, wherever it appears in a sentence, is always a capital letter.**

2. **Capital letters are used for *proper nouns*, that is, for the particular names of people, places, countries or things.**
Example:

James Joyce
United States of America
Pacific Ocean
Jamaica

When the names of rivers, oceans, mountain ranges and so on, consist of more than one word, both words are capitalised.

In foreign names, capitals are not used for words such as *de, di, du* except occasionally when a foreign name has been anglicised (adopted into the English language).
Example:

Tierra del Fuego and *Rio de Janeiro*

Capital letters are also used in a religious context to refer to God, Jesus, The Bible and its books, the Holy Koran and other scriptures.

Points of the compass are only capitalised when they are part of the name of a country, city or geographic region.

The words *north, south, east* and *west* are not given capital letters when they are used as nouns or adjectives.
Example:

We say: On the north side of town...
but: North America

3. **Capital letters are used for the days of the week and the months of the year. Seasons do not begin with a capital letter.**
Example:

In the summer, we are going to America for our holiday.
but: On the first Thursday in July, we are flying to America.

4. **Describing words, formed from proper nouns, are usually spelt with a capital letter.**
Example:

The French people in Paris drive fast.
The English are well-known as animal lovers.

However, when the describing word formed from a proper noun names a common object, small letters are used.
Example:

        There are brussel sprouts, french apples and swiss cheese on the menu.

There are exceptions. These include:

        The Bunsen burner, the Liebig condenser, the Davy lamp.

These tend to retain the name of the inventor and so maintain a capital letter for that part of the name.

5. The main words in the title of a book, play, T.V. programme or film always begin with a capital letter.

In a title, small words like *the* or *an* or *a* do not have a capital letter unless they are the first word of the title.
Example:

Wind *in the* Willows

The Adventures *of the* Three Musketeers

6. At the beginning of each line of poetry use a capital letter.

Example:

But pleasures are like poppies spread:
You seize the flow'r, its bloom is shed.

7. Each word in an address begins with a capital letter.

Example:

Owls Hoot,
Mill Close,
Brancaster.

8. Initials and many abbreviations are written in capital letters.

Example:

J.R.Wilson Esq., B.Sc., M.Phil.
B.B.C., I.T.V. and Carlton are T.V. companies.

The punctuation of abbreviations and initials is discussed in a later section in this book.

Titles are given capital letters when they refer to a specific person, that is when the title could be replaced by an *actual* proper name, but use small letters when the title is used generally.
Example:

      The Prime Minister of Great Britain lives at 10, Downing Street, London.
       At the conference there were prime ministers and presidents from many countries.

9. The first word spoken in direct speech always begins with a capital letter.

Example:

      Sara asked, "Will you go shopping with me, James?"

PRACTICE : CAPITAL LETTERS

There are 10 uses of the capital letter:

1. **At the beginning of a sentence.**
2. **For the pronoun *I*.**
3. **For proper nouns, religious words and points of the compass when they are part of a name.**
4. **For the days of the week and months of the year.**
5. **Describing words formed from proper nouns.**
6. **The main words of the title of a book, play, T.V. programme etc.**
7. **At the beginning of each line of poetry.**
8. **For each word in an address.**
9. **Initials and many abbreviations are written in capital letters.**
10. **The first word spoken in direct speech is always a capital letter.**

Exercise Six: _____

Write out the sentences below inserting a capital letter wherever one is needed.

1. the french president is visiting london next september.

2. nicholas and jason go to fairfield middle school.

3. i went to see the film 'denis' at the tower cinema last thursday.

4. michael is going to paris, france, on a school trip in july.

5. gemma's aunt janet is vising her in norwich, this summer.

6. m.p. stands for member of parliament, p.m. for prime minister.

7. brian wants to drive his porsche to germany.

8. james and i went to visit windsor castle to see the queen.

9. sara has read 'the animals of farthing wood' and 'the wind in the willows'.

10. i went with bernard to see barry at kingston general hospital.

FINAL PUNCTUATION MARKS

There are *three* punctuation marks that can end a sentence:

     a.   **A full stop (.)**

     b.   **A question mark (?)**

     c.   **An exclamation mark (!)**

A *question* mark and an *exclamation* mark take the place of a full stop and must be followed by a capital letter.

When is each used?

This may depend upon the type of sentence you are punctuating.

TYPES OF SENTENCE

There are four main types of sentence:

There are those that make a **declaration** or **statement** about something.

Example:

The wind is blowing.

It is Friday today.

Each sentence states a fact, is called a **statement** and *ends in a full stop.*

A *full stop* (.) also ends a command or imperative. A **command** or **imperative** orders, requires or compels.

Example:

Close that door.

Open your exercise book.

Turn to page forty-nine.

A full stop (.) is used at the end of a statement and a command.

THE QUESTION MARK

A *question mark (?)* comes at the end of a sentence which asks a **question**.

This is called the **interrogative**. If the sentence you hear requires an answer, it is a question.

Example:

Will you come to my house after school tonight?

This sentence requires an answer. It is therefore, a question.

Do not confuse that sentence with this:

Example:

David asked if he was in the football team this week.

This sentence does not ask a question and does not require a question mark. It is a statement. It is reporting what David asked.

A question mark comes at the end of a question.
Use a question mark only at the end of the words actually spoken.

Example:

"Am I in the football team this week?" asked David.

These words were actually spoken by David, they ask a question, they require a question mark.

THE EXCLAMATION MARK

The third type of final punctuation mark, the *exclamation mark* (!), follows:
a sharp expression of strong emotion, often surprise or astonishment, or a warning.
Often these expressions are exclaimed, said loudly, shouted or stressed.
Occasionally an exclamation mark indicates a statement which should not be taken too seriously, that it is either meant as humour or perhaps sarcasm.

An exclamation mark (!) takes the place of a full stop at the end of an **exclamatory** sentence and must be followed by a capital letter. It may come at the end of a full sentence, or indeed, may follow only one word.
Example:

Ouch! That hurt!
Get off the grass immediately!

It is often up to you to decide when to use an exclamation mark.
Example:

I just love that yellow sweater!
I just love that yellow sweater.

The same sentence above has been written twice: once with an exclamation mark and once with a full stop.
The choice of final punctuation mark depends on the tone in which the words are delivered, the way in which the words are expressed, the effect the author wants to make on the reader.
The first sentence suggests a statement that should not be taken too seriously, is probably denoting *sarcasm*. The exclamation mark would help the reader to interpret this tone. The reader would detect the sarcastic underlying attitude of the speaker simply from the presence of the exclamation mark.

The second sentence is a statement of fact, *I just love that yellow sweater*.
This therefore, requires a full stop only. The punctuation tells us there is no underlying tone or expression of sarcasm.

Similarly, something unusual in the streets of a city may cause surprise and hence require an exclamation mark. The same sight may only require a full stop if it is commonplace or expected.
Example:
>   I've just seen a baboon swinging through the trees.

This would require an exclamation mark if you are standing on the high street of Croydon, but only a full stop if you were either in London Zoo or the wooded regions of Africa.

However, a golden rule is:
Use the exclamation mark sparingly. Use it to create effect, tone and interest in a piece of free writing.
Use it here:
>   Rex! Come here!

Avoid using an exclamation mark when it is not necessary or evident.
Avoid it here:
>   I'm going to school today.

Indeed, to use an exclamation mark where one should not be used, can give the wrong impression.
Example:
>   It was lovely having you to stay for the weekend!
>   You don't eat much!

Was it lovely? Does she eat much? Might the exclamation mark suggest to the reader that the writer does not quite mean what he appears to be saying? Take care!

Never use more than one exclamation mark at the end of a sentence.
Never use a combination of question marks and exclamation marks.
Example:
This is wrong: Who do you think you are?!?!

However, there are three occasions when an exclamation mark **must** be used:
Always use an exclamation mark:

1. **At the end of a sentence which begins with the word *what* or *how* and which does not ask a question.**
Such sentences usually denote expressions of strong emotion.
Example:
>   What an idiot you are!
>   How clever you are!

2. **Short or sudden exclamations standing by themselves require an exclamation mark.**
Example:
>   Watch out!
>   Help!

You have a choice of punctuation here. You can make the single exclamation part of the full sentence, in which case the exclamation mark will go to the end of the full sentence and the exclamation will be separated from the rest of the sentence by a comma. Like this:

Look out, you've just killed the cat!

Or, two exclamation marks can be used. Like this:

Look out! You've just killed the cat!

Be careful to begin the second sentence with a capital letter.

This is **not** correct:

Look out! you've just killed the cat!

Here, *you've* begins with a small letter. In this case, a comma must take the place of the first exclamation mark as in the first example above.

Either punctuation is acceptable.

C. A name called by itself and not as part of a sentence is followed by an exclamation mark.

Example:

Sam! Stop teasing the cat!

Sam, stop teasing the cat!

Again you have the same choice of punctuation as in B above. Sam followed by a comma, can be treated as part of one full sentence, in which case the exclamation mark comes at the end of the full sentence. Or, as above, two separate sentences, each with an exclamation mark of their own, *each sentence beginning with a capital letter*, is acceptable.

PRACTICE : FINAL PUNCTUATION MARKS

There are *three* punctuation marks that can end a sentence:

    a.   **A full stop (.)**
    b.   **A question mark (?)**
    c.   **An exclamation mark (!)**

A *full stop* (.) is used at the end of a *statement* and a *command*.

A *question mark* (?) comes at the end of a *question*.
Use a question mark only at the end of the words actually spoken.

An *exclamation mark* (!) is used at the end of a sharp expression **of emotion, often surprise, astonishment, sarcasm or humour.**
An exclamation is often said loudly, shouted or stressed.
Always use an exclamation mark:
    1. At the end of sentences beginning with *how* or *what* which do not ask a question.
    2. A sharp or sudden exclamation standing by itself.
    3. A name called by itself and not as part of a sentence.
A *question* mark and an *exclamation* mark take the place of a full stop and must be followed by a capital letter.

Exercise Seven: _____

Some of the sentences below are *questions* and require a question mark at the end. Others are *statements* or *commands* and require a full stop only. Rewrite each sentence punctuating each sentence correctly.

1. What time is it It's time you went to bed

2. He asked what time it was Why does he need to know

3. Jenny asked how much the dress cost

4. Nicky asked the little girl if she was lost

5. Where can I get an interesting book

6. James wondered what time Khaled would come

7. Dale and Liam want to know what they're having for tea

8. What is the capital of Egypt

9. Don't you ask a lot of questions

10. Can't you close the back door behind you

Exercise Eight: _____

Rewrite each sentence adding the correct punctuation mark at the end of these sentences. Each sentence ends in a *full stop*, *question mark* or *exclamation mark*.

1. What a hot day Do you want to swim I think it would be glorious

2. Gosh Have you seen her hair It's bright purple I think she's overdone it this time

3. How silly You've got your clothes wet How did you do that

4. Sam Stop What an idiot you are You've just backed into that Mercedes

5. I have to ask if you can drive It strikes me you still need lessons

6. What time is it I'm supposed to be at Samantha's house by seven o'clock

7. What a clumsy girl you are Didn't you see the ink Now it's all over the carpet

8. Did you ask if you were in the team this week He said you should ask him

9. Thank goodness, it's Friday I can stay in bed in the morning

10. Are you going camping this summer We need to ask if we can come

THE FULL STOP USED IN INITIALS AND ABBREVIATIONS

Initials and words which have been abbreviated are usually followed by a full stop.
Example:
Initials used for a person's name:

> Mr J.D.Walker.
> Mrs S.T.Brown.

Abbreviations:

> M.P.(Member of Parliament)   B.B.C.(British Broadcasting Corporation)
> Ph.D.(Doctor of Philosophy)   B.Sc.(Bachelor of Science)
> e.g.(example)   v.i.p.(very important person)
> i.e.(that is)   m.p.g.(miles per gallon)

adj.(adjective), pl.(plural), etc.(etcetera), n.(noun), info.(information), v.(versus), min.(minute), sing.(singular), geog.(geography), Aug.(August), yrs.(years).

1. Only use capital letters in abbreviations where there would be one in the actual word. *August* would be abbreviated *Aug.*, *Monday*, *Mon.* and so on, but *s.a.e* for *stamped addressed envelope*, would not need capital letters.

2. Full stops are often used as abbreviation marks where the final portion of the word has been omitted as can be seen in many of the examples above.

3. Where the first and the last letter of a word is used as the abbreviation, the full stop is *tending* to disappear as in such abbreviations as Dr for Doctor, Mr for Mister and St for Street or Saint.

4. There is also a *tendency* nowadays to leave out the full stop in very well known abbreviations such as BBC and ITV.

However, if you are ever not sure whether an abbreviation needs a full stop or not, put one in and be safe. Points 3 and 4 above are only *tendencies*. It is still correct to use a full stop as an abbreviation mark for most abbreviations.

5. Some abbreviations have gradually become accepted as real words, such as NASA (North American Space Agency) and OPEC (Organisation of Petroleum-Exporting Countries). We call these *acronyms*.

6. Also, where an abbreviated word such as *gym* for gymnasium, *vet* for veterinary surgeon, and *ad* or *advert* for advertisement has become widely accepted into common usage, the full stop has been omitted.

7. However, we certainly **do not** need to use a full stop after an abbreviated mathematical unit or for decimal currency.

Example:

> We say   *cm* for *centimetres*   *km* for *kilometres*
>   *ins* for *inches*   *kg* for *kilograms*
>   £ for pound   *p* for new pence

Decimal currency and mathematical units do not require a full stop.

Finally, an important point to note when you are following an initial or an abbreviation with a full stop is that it does not affect any other punctuation in a

sentence. A full stop can and should be immediately followed by another punctuation mark such as a comma, semi-colon, question or exclamation mark. Though strictly accurate to have two full stops when the abbreviated word comes at the end of a sentence, there is a *tendency* not to follow a full stop belonging to an abbreviation with a full stop belonging to the end of a sentence. In other words, the full stop following the abbreviated word *tends* to serve also as the final full stop.
Example:

The M.P. with a Ph.D. went to the B.B.C.

but   Has the M.P. for Bournemouth seen the P.M.?

Other uses of the full stop:
Usually three full stops are used to indicate the omission of a word or words.
A full stop or a succession of three full stops can be used as *omission marks*, to show that something is missing, or withheld or that the sentence or quotation is tailing off in an incomplete way. If these three dots come at the end of the sentence, one dot represents the full stop.
Example:

There was a loud bang and then silence. She waited and waited...

'To be or not to be...' I've forgotten it!

PRACTICE : THE FULL STOP IN INITIALS AND ABBREVIATIONS

Initials and abbreviations are usually followed by a full stop except an abbreviated mathematical unit and decimal currency. All other punctuation in the sentence remains the same.

Three dots can be used to show *omission* of a word or words.

Exercise Nine: _____

Write out the sentences below inserting a capital letter and a full stop wherever one is needed.

1.   roald dahl wrote the 'bfg', 'witches', 'boy...' i've forgotten the others

2.   the mp for hull is barry brocklehurst

3.   there are ten mm in one cm

4.   in the dictionary it said happiness n, happy adj i know what that means

5.   august (aug) and september (sept) are the eighth and ninth months of the year

6.   there are 100p in £1

7.   put the tv on there's a good programme on the bbc

8.   knives, forks, spoons etc are called cutlery

9.   hot countries, eg africa, are often dry

10. the plural (pl) of knife (sing) is knives

THE COMMA

A comma (,) should never be used as a full stop. Whilst a comma, like a full stop, separates words or groups of words from each other, the comma is found *inside the sentence* and is less definite, not as strong or as *final* as a full stop. A comma designates a pause, a breath, a slight division between different parts of the sentence, an indication of a small break in the continuity before the topic of the sentence continues. A full stop on the other hand, separates sentences, and by so doing, may separate ideas or topics.

There are 16 uses of the comma.

These 16 uses of the comma are broken up into five sections. Each section has several uses of the comma explained followed by Practice Exercises.

1.   Commas are used to separate items in a list or series. The comma takes the place of the word *and* or *or*.
Example:
Instead of writing:
     John had a pencil and a pen and a ruler and an exercise book in his bag.

We should write:
     John had a pencil, a pen, a ruler and an exercise book in his bag.

Note that the final *and* is not replaced by a comma and therefore remains with no punctuation mark around it.
After all, the comma *replaces* the word *and* or similar conjunction. The final *and* is not usually replaced, so a comma is not required.

The list may be of separate items (things), actions, or groups of words.
Example:
Sally ate an apple, an orange, a banana, a pear and a chocolate biscuit before being sick.   (separate items)

Don't shout, speak, run, jump about or make any disturbance whilst the exam is in progress.   (separate actions)

Please iron the shirts, clean the kitchen, tidy your bedroom and make some lunch before you leave.   (separate groups of words)

In the examples above the commas separate different items in a list. It is evident that an *apple* and an *orange* are separate, different items.

Where the adjectives in a list convey a single thought or idea, it is acceptable to leave out the commas.
Example:

> A great big dog came bounding into the garden and tipped over the barbeque.
> The bright red car came speeding into the car park.

In the first example, the words *great* and *big* convey a single idea. They are not independent adjectives as such, but rather qualifiers of the noun *dog*.
Similarly, in the second example, the words *bright red car* convey a single thought. It would therefore, be quite acceptable to leave out the commas in these sentences. However, take care! If ever you are unsure, put in a comma!

2. When speaking to, or addressing a person, that person's name, status or title, is separated from the rest of the sentence by a comma.
It does not matter whether the *term of address* or person's name is at the beginning of the sentence, in the middle of the sentence or at the end of the sentence. In each case it is separated from the other words in the sentence by commas.

To do that may require one comma if the *term of address* or name is at the beginning of the sentence, two commas if it occurs in the middle of the sentence, or one comma and a full stop if it is at the end of the sentence.
Example:
At the beginning of a sentence:

> James, please turn off the television.

In the middle of the sentence:

> Please, James, turn off the television.

At the end of the sentence:

> Please turn off the television, James.

In all these examples, *James* is being spoken to, or addressed, by name, so his name is separated from the other words in the sentence by commas.
This rule is used when you are speaking to someone directly.
Do not confuse this rule with the following example:

> Christopher, please show Emma the kittens.

Here, Emma's name is not separated from the rest of the sentence by commas because Emma is not being spoken *to*, only spoken *about*. Christopher, however, is being spoken *to*. Christopher's name, then, is the only one where a comma is necessary to separate his name from the other words in the sentence.

3. When *yes, no, well, please* or *thank you* is part of an answer, a comma or commas, is used to separate these words from the rest of the sentence.
Example:

> Yes, Sara and Christopher can go swimming today.
> Well, I hope you will take care.
> No, I do not mind at all, thank you.

Take care! Do not separate these words from other words in the sentence when they are part of *reported* speech.
Example:

> Timmy always remembers to say thank you for a present.

4. Use a comma to separate question phrases which are added on to the end of a sentence.
Example:

> You are coming, aren't you?
> You do like sprouts, don't you?

PRACTICE 1 : THE COMMA

There are 16 uses of the comma. Here are the first four uses.

A comma or commas are used:
1. **To separate items in a list or series.**
2. **In a term of address,**
    that is, when we are calling someone by name.
3. **When *yes, no, well, please* or *thank you* is part of a**
    spoken answer.
4. **To separate *question phrases* such as *aren't you?* and**
    ***don't you?* which are added on to the end of a sentence.**

Exercise Ten: _____

Rewrite the following sentences which Practise Rule One above and are concerned with *lists*. Replace each *and* or *or* (except the last one), with a comma.

1. Sandra ate an apple and an orange and a whole grapefruit this evening.

2. Lee has worked in a newsagent and a hospital and a garage as part of his 'Work Experience'.

3. Anderson and Hardy and Owen must report to Mr. Jones immediately.

4. A big furry cat with long white whiskers has just walked across the lawn.

5. He kicked the ball hard and low and fast straight into the hands of the waiting goal-keeper.

6. Ice-skating and swimming and dancing are my favourite pastimes.

7. Please tidy your room and make your bed and walk the dog before you go to bed.

8. The old man had a brown and well-weathered and wrinkled face.

9.   A pilot must learn to climb and bank and roll and stall his plane.

10. Pick up the bucket and spade and the wet swimming clothes and the picnic basket and the newspaper.

Exercise Eleven: _____

Put a comma or commas into the correct places in these sentences.
These sentences practise Rule Two above and are concerned with *addressing a person.*

1.   Please Miss I need to go to the cloakroom.

2.   Stuart pass me that book.

3.   Will you Caroline show Miss Jones where to go?

4.   I say Miss Hardy that's a pretty dress you are wearing.

5.   When do I take the medicine Dr Cooper?

6.   Fido stop chasing the cat!

7.   Michael go to bed at once!

8.   I haven't got a pencil sir.

9.   Alice and Fred want to go too Mary.

10. Take Nicholas to Mr. Smith's room at once Jonathan.

Exercise Twelve:_____

Try combining some of your skills here. The sentences below need capital letters, final punctuation marks and commas as in listing or addressing a person (uses 1 and 2). Copy out each sentence, punctuating it carefully. Sometimes there is 1, sometimes 2 and sometimes 3 sentences in each question.

1.   pick up your bicycle james and put it in the shed next to the lawnmower secateurs and garden shears

2.   I beg your pardon sir but I left the books pens pencils and rulers on your desk

3.   tonight my friends is a special occasion it is the shared birthday party of susan maureen and hilary happy birthday girls

4.   sir the french teacher has asked barry and I to go to the staffroom to carry some books may we be excused

5.   my sister has had measles mumps and chicken pox and she's only eight

6. good evening ladies and gentlemen in front of you there should be paper a pencil and a pen shall we proceed with the first item on the agenda

7. gosh sam what have you got you were asked to get two tins of beans a packet of biscuits and a loaf of bread

8. the hardest working most diligent and keenest person I know sam is you

9. I wonder what jo is doing do you think he is alright sue

10. stop stop exactly where you are what are you boys doing speak boy speak i'm asking you a question

Exercise Thirteen: _____

Put capital letters, final punctuation marks and commas in the correct places in these sentences. All four uses of the comma as summarised above are included. Ignore the need for speech marks.

1. sara have you see the film 'jurassic park' my brother david was a bit frightened by the dinosaurs weren't you david

2. well I never you've eaten up all your cabbage you said you didn't like cabbage didn't you

3. sally made the sandwiches packed the cool box put it in the car and set off in great excitement she spent most of the day in a traffic jam

4. follow me men we need to hide go around that tree through the hedge over the stile and down the bank they'll never see us there

5. Operator i've been cut off can you help me I was talking to my aunt when the line went dead oh thank you that's better

6. you can manage that big bag of shopping can't you well thank you young man that's very kind of you

5. A pair of commas is used to separate words or groups of words which are not absolutely necessary to the meaning of the sentence.

A.   When the group of words begins with *who, which, whom* or *whose* and is not absolutely necessary to the meaning of the sentence, commas are used to mark off the words from the rest of the sentence.

Example:
> Nicholas, who likes to ride his bike to school, is in Mr Cooper's class.

Here we are talking about Nicholas. We make two separate observations about him, that:
      a.   he likes to ride his bike to school, and
      b.   he is in Mr Cooper's class.

These statements are not dependent on each other - the fact that *Nicholas is in Mr Cooper's class* is quite a separate issue to him enjoying *riding his bike to school*.

We do not need *who likes to ride his bike to school* to identify *who* we are talking about here - we already know. This extra bit of information is not essential to, and adds nothing to the meaning of the sentence.
Indeed, *who likes to ride his bike to school* could quite easily be left out of the sentence and we would still know *who* we are talking about.
Nicholas is in Mr Cooper's class.
We need no further information about Nicholas to understand the sentence. We therefore separate the words *who likes to ride his bike to school* from the other words in the sentence by commas.

Commas are used to separate the *extra information* about Nicholas away from the main topic of the sentence. Instead of using the word Nicholas twice, the relative pronoun, *who* is used.

What we are really doing here is linking two sentences together using the word *who*, which is a relative pronoun, in place of the antecedent, *Nicholas*, to achieve it. If we were to substitute the word *Nicholas* for the word *who*, each group of words could easily stand as a sentence in its own right. We are simply linking them together with the use of commas to give the reader a bit of *extra information* about Nicholas. The sentence would make perfectly good sense, we would know exactly *who* we are talking about, if the words marked off by commas were missed out completely.

Non-Restrictive Relative Clauses. For those who need more information.
Nicholas is in Mr Cooper's class is the *main clause* of the sentence and as such could stand alone as a sentence and make complete sense. *Who likes to ride a bike to school* is a *non-restrictive* or *non-defining relative clause*. It is a *relative clause* because it begins with the *relative pronoun, who*. It is *non-restrictive (non-defining)* because the clause itself does not tell us *who* we are talking about. There again, it does not need to tell us *who* we are talking about because we already know. *It simply adds information about the person or thing already identified.*

Where the relative clause is simply adding more information to the sentence, commas are used to separate it from the main clause.

Example:
Kingstown High School, which has fifty classrooms, is outside the town.

Here the relative pronoun *which* is used in place of the antecedent *Kingstown High School*. *Which has fifty classrooms* adds nothing and is not essential to the meaning of the sentence. It is not pointing out for us *which school?* We already know. The words *which has fifty classrooms* is simply adding *more information* and should be separated from the rest of the sentence by a pair of commas.

In a *non-defining* or *non-retsrictive* clause we always use the relative pronoun *who* when we are talking about a *person* and *which* when we are talking about a *thing*. We cannot use *that*. We can also use *whose* when we talk about *possession*.
Example:

> Jo Bloggs, whose brother is a friend of mine, goes to my school.

A group of words beginning with the word *who, that* or *which* that is essential to the meaning of the sentence is not separated from the other words in the sentence by commas.

Commas are used to mark off the words which are **not** absolutely essential to the meaning of the sentence. Sometimes the group of words beginning with the word *who, which, that* or *whose*, **is essential** to the meaning of the sentence.
When the group of words is essential, commas are not used.
Example:

> A car that stalls is of little use.

Which car? The *one that stalls*.

> An athlete who trains can perform well.

Which athlete? The *one who trains*.

> A house whose windows are broken is draughty.

Which house? The *one with broken windows*.

In all these examples we need the group of words beginning with *that, who* and *whose* to make sense of what we are talking about. Each group of words is essential to the meaning of the sentence. We cannot set them apart from the other words in the sentence with commas as if they did not matter.

In the first example, if we remove *that stalls*, we are left with the words *A car is of little use*. This is clearly incomplete. We need the words *that stalls* to tell us *which car?*

In the second example, if we remove *who trains*, we are left with the words *An athlete performs well*. Which athlete performs well? We need the information *who trains* to understand the sentence.

In the third example if we remove the words *whose windows are broken*, we are left with *A house is draughty*. Which house is draughty? Only by leaving the words *whose windows are broken,* do we know. Commas therefore are not used.

In all these sentences then, the words beginning with *who, whose* and *that* are essential to the meaning and cannot be separated from the rest of the sentence by commas.

Restrictive Relative Clauses.   For those who need more information.
With reference to the first example above: *A car that stalls is of little use.* Here the relative clause *that stalls* is a *restrictive* (sometimes called *defining*) *relative clause*.

Relative because it begins with a *relative pronoun, that, restrictive (defining)*, because it tells us *which car* the author means. Without *that stalls*, we would not know *which car* the author is talking about. This time the relative clause is essential to the meaning of the sentence. Indeed, without it the sentence becomes meaningless. In this case, the relative clause is not separated from the rest of the sentence by commas but is an essential part of the sentence and cannot be moved to one side as unimportant.

In a *restrictive relative clause* we use *who* for people and *that* or *which* for things.

Compare:

> Sara, who likes to read, is a good girl.
> The person who woke Sara was a burglar.

In the first example, the phrase *who likes to read* is not absolutely essential to the meaning of the sentence. We know *which girl* is a good girl without the words *who likes to read*. A pair of commas then is used to separate these words from the rest of the sentence.

Here, *who likes to read* is a *non-defining (non-restrictive) relative clause* and can be separated from the rest of the sentence using commas because it is not essential to the meaning.

In the second example, *who woke Sara* **is essential** to the meaning of the sentence, indeed, without these words, the reader would not know *who* the burglar was - he was the one who woke Sara!
If we take out the words *who woke Sara*, we would be left with
> *The person was a burglar.*

The reaction of the reader would be to ask *which person was a burglar?* Answer, the person who woke Sara!
Without the phrase *who woke Sara* the reader does not know *who* the author is talking about.

This is a *defining (restrictive) relative clause* because it tells us *which person*. Without it the sentence is meaningless. It cannot be separated from the remaining part of the sentence using commas.

Example:

> Uncle Harold said that the dog which barked very loudly
> in the neighbour's garden woke him.

Here we do not use commas. All the words are essential to the meaning of the sentence. The phrase beginning *which* cannot be separated from the other words is the sentence. After all, we only know which dog woke up Uncle Harold from the whole sentence!

If we know *who* or *what* is meant without the additional information, the group of words is not absolutely necessary to the meaning of the sentence and we *can* separate them from the rest of the sentence by commas.

If, however, we do not know *who* or *what* is meant without the additional information, such information is essential to the meaning of the sentence and a pair of commas is not needed.
Example:

> The boy who rides the yellow bike is my friend.

Do you need to know the boy *rides a yellow bike* to understand *which boy* the author is talking about?
> Yes.
> Does this sentence require commas?
> No, there should **not** be any commas in this sentence. Without *who rides a yellow bike* we would not know *who* the friend is. This information is essential to the meaning of the sentence. Commas are not necessary.

> Michael who rides a yellow bike is my friend.

Do you need the information regarding *riding a yellow bike* to know who the author's friend is?
> No.
> Does this sentence require commas?
> Yes. We know his friend is Michael. There should be commas around *who rides a yellow bike*. Here the words are not absolutely necessary to the meaning of the sentence. We can understand the sentence without them. We must therefore, separate them from the other words in the sentence using commas.

> Michael, who rides a yellow bike, is my friend.

B.   We use commas around a group of words which begins with a word ending in *ing* or *ed* and which is not absolutely necessary to the meaning of the sentence.

Participle Clauses.   For those who need more information.
We call such a group of words as this a *participle clause* because the *participle* of the verb is being used - either the *present participle*, ending in *ing*, or the *past participle*, ending in *ed*. (See *Grammar Rules and Practice 2* for more information.)
Example:

> Andrew, *dribbling the ball magnificently*, ran past the opposition.

Here the group of words beginning with a word ending in *ing*, dribbl*ing*, is not absolutely essential to the meaning of the sentence and is separated from the other words in the sentence by commas.
These words could come at the beginning of a sentence, in which case only one comma is necessary:

> *Dribbling the ball magnificently*, Andrew ran past the opposition.

or at the end of the sentence using one comma and the final punctuation mark to separate the words from the rest of the sentence:

> Andrew ran past the opposition, *dribbling the ball magnificently*.

Example:

Michael, *dressed smartly in his scout uniform*, left for camp.
Dressed smartly in his scout uniform, Michael left for camp.
Michael left for camp, *dressed smartly in his scout uniform*.

Here, the words *dressed smartly in his scout uniform* are not absolutely necessary to the meaning of the sentence and are separated from the other words in the sentence using commas. This time the first word ends in *ed*, dress*ed*.
As shown above, this group of words can be written at the beginning, in the middle or at the end of the sentence.

C.   The words marked off by commas may be used as description of the main topic of the sentence.
Example:

My best friend, Susan, has brown hair.

My best friend and *Susan* is the same person. *Susan* is another way of describing *my best friend*. They are interchangeable. The word *Susan* is not absolutely necessary to the meaning of the sentence and could be left out.

My best friend has brown hair.
Susan has brown hair.

Commas, therefore, are used to separate these descriptive words from the main topic.

Example:

London, the capital of England, is a very interesting city.

The capital of England is being used to describe *London*. The sentence would still make complete sense without the words *the capital of England*.
Commas are therefore used to separate it from the other words in the sentence.

Usually a word or group of words which is used in this way, comes immediately next to the person, place or thing it describes.

PRACTICE 2 : THE COMMA

Use a comma or commas to separate groups of words from the rest of the sentence:

5.   When information is given which is not absolutely necessary to the meaning of the sentence. These may be classified:
   a.   when the group of words begins with *who, which, whose*, or *whom*.
   b.   when the first word of the group of words ends in *ed* or *ing*.
   c.   when the group of words is used as description.

Exercise Fourteen: _____

Read through each sentence below to decide which groups of words beginning with the word *who,*
which, that or *whose* **are necessary** for the meaning of the sentence to be complete. Place a **tick**
against those sentences.
Put a cross against those sentences where the groups of words beginning with *who, which, whom* and
whose **are not absolutely necessary** for the meaning of the sentence to be complete.

Rewrite the sentences placing commas where necessary.

1.   I would like you all to make Mrs. Williams who is coming to speak to us this afternoon
     very welcome.

2.   James Bowey who owns a new mountain bike is in my class.

3.   The car that broke down is being towed to the garage.

4.   I went to fill the car which had run out of petrol.

5.   Mary who had the clearest voice was given the leading role in the play.

6.   Blenheim Palace which the class visited last summer is near Oxford.

7.   A boy who has a hobby will not be bored.

8.   My brother Mark who is in the army is coming home for Christmas.

9.   A pen that won't write is of little use.

10. Sally whose brother is a pop singer is my best friend.

Exercise Fifteen: _____

This Exercise is the same as the one above.
Read through each sentence below to decide which groups of words beginning with the word *who,*
which, that or *whose* **are necessary** for the meaning of the sentence to be complete. Place a **tick**
against those sentences.
Put a cross against those sentences where the groups of words beginning with *who, which, whom* and
whose **are not absolutely necessary** for the meaning of the sentence to be complete.

Rewrite the sentences placing commas where necessary.

1.   Will the boy who threw that piece of chalk please own up.

2.   We go to Norfolk which is a lovely part of the country for our holidays.

3.   Jane collected the suit which had been taken for drycleaning.

4.   The china plate which already had a crack in it broke when I dropped it.

5.   The village store which sells everything from crisps to crockery is run by Mrs Bailey.

6. Is there anybody here who can hear me?

7. I have not yet seen Dr. Davis who is our new form teacher.

8. Will the person who parked a red sports car in front of the gates remove it at once?

9. This is the road that goes to town.

10. A student who works hard for his examinations will do well.

Exercise Sixteen: _____

Each of the sentences below contains a group of words beginning with a word which ends in *ing* or *ed*, which tells us more about something but which is not absolutely necessary to the meaning of the sentence. Write out each sentence, underlining the group of words and setting it apart from the other words in the sentence by a comma or commas.

1. Trying to be helpful Brenda only made things worse.

2. Blowing up the balloon Simon looked like a fat-cheeked little elf.

3. Peter sobbing uncontrollably could hardly speak.

4. Tired of her independence Carol came home.

5. Stumbling along the path the tired and hungry scouts were looking for shelter.

6. Mr. Harding losing his temper shouted at the class.

7. Maureen set off for her first dance dressed in her prettiest dress.

8. Feeling rather ill he stumbled to the telephone.

9. The apples falling off the tree were collected by the children below.

10. Chuckling quietly to himself David left the room.

Exercise Seventeen: _____

Each of the sentences below contains a group of words which describes what goes immediately before it. Write out each sentence, underlining this group of words and setting it apart from the other words in the sentence using a comma or commas.

1. Shaun my nephew is an excellent driver.

2. The class was surprised when Michael Higgins a disruptive student was made a prefect.

3. Mrs. Kaye our neighbour kindly offered to look after the kittens while we were on holiday.

4. 'Spindrift' the largest boat in the harbour was damaged in the storm.

5. Liam a tall boy for his age began school today.

6. His car a blue sports car travels fast.

7. Vesuvius the famous volcano is in Italy.

8. The headmaster introduced Mr. Hicks the guest speaker.

9. My neices Jessica and Jade are going with us.

10. They spent their holidays in Gstaad a mountain resort.

Exercise Eighteen: _____

This Exercise practises the three Rules you have just been studying. Place the comma or commas correctly in the following sentences.

1. The girl who lives next door is in my class.

2. Leaving early he beat the traffic.

3. The ice-cream which we bought was so soft it melted before we could eat it.

4. Thinking quickly Jeanne delivered the argument that won the debate for her team.

5. Tom Carpenter form captain took the assembly today.

6. The train which was empty was on its way to London.

7. Dressed smartly in his new suit he left for the interview.

8. The bird with the worm arrived early.

9. Mr Higgins our form teacher likes reading books.

10. Arthur the football coach worked hard for the team.

6. There are specific words or groups of words we always separate from the rest of the sentence by a comma.

Words such as:

however,	therefore,	meanwhile,	well,
by the way,	without doubt,	moreover,	nevertheless.

Example:

> *Nevertheless*, I shall go to the dance.
> I shall go, *nevertheless*, to the dance.
> I shall go to the dance, *nevertheless*.

The particular word can go at the beginning, in the middle or at the end of the sentence. Each time it is separated from the other words in the sentence by a comma, commas, or one comma and a full stop depending, as can be seen above, where it is found in the sentence. Whilst it is *usual* always to separate these words using commas, you have some choice when the word occurs *in the middle* or *at the end* of the sentence. To say:

He was, *meanwhile*, late for class.
He was *meanwhile* late for class.

I shall be there, *nevertheless*.
I shall be there *nevertheless*.

is a matter of personal preference. To use commas or not - either punctuation is acceptable and correct.

Take care! If you use the word *however* in this context:
However bad the weather, we must still go by car.
a comma after *however* is not necessary.

7. **Other words or groups of words (such as *outside, inside, in the morning, in the main*) may need to be followed by a comma, to avoid ambiguity.**
Example:
Outside, the playground was noisy.
To put a comma after *outside* would prevent the reader reading this sentence as
Outside the playground...
In the main, discipline must be upheld.
Avoids being read as *In the main discipline...*
Naturally, he was very pleased.
Avoids reading *Naturally he...*

Also, as we saw in the section on the exclamation mark:
8. **A comma can be used to separate exclamations when they are part of a sentence. A comma in these cases, takes the place of an exclamation mark.**
Example:
Oh! What a pity you did that!

becomes

Oh, what a pity you did that!

PRACTICE 3 : THE COMMA

> **6.** **Specific words such as *however* and *meanwhile* are separated from the rest of the sentence by a comma.**
> **7.** **Other words may be separated to avoid ambiguity.**
> **8.** **Exclamations, when they are part of a sentence, are separated from the rest of the sentence by a comma.**

Exercise Nineteen: _____

Write out the following sentences adding commas where you feel they are necessary.

1. It was without doubt the worst restaurant I had ever been in.

2. I wonder by the way if you could tell me the way to the city centre?

3. She agreed to go however.

4. Naturally I would love to go.

5. Oh I say that looks super!

6. He was nevertheless determined to go.

7. We shall meet again no doubt.

8. It is therefore my privelege to open this new library.

9. Well I must be going now.

10. By the way do you remember her?

9. **Groups of words beginning with words such as *when, after, before, until, while, since, if, unless, although, though* and *because*, are separated from the remaining part of the sentence by a comma or commas if they come at the beginning or in the middle of the sentence. However, no comma is necessary if the same group of words comes at the end of the sentence.**

Main and Subordinate Clauses.   For those who need more information.
Complex sentences, which contain two different groups of words, can be thought of as being in two parts. The main part, which we call the *main clause*, and the part which depends on the main clause, which we call the *subordinate clause*. You have a choice which part to put at the beginning of the sentence. Commas are used to separate these two parts if you choose to put the *subordinate clause* first or in the middle of the sentence. If it remains at the end of the sentence and the main clause comes first, no comma is necessary.
Here, the subordinate clause has been italicised.
Example:
> *If you wash the car for me*, I'll give you some pocket-money.
>   but
> I'll give you some pocket money *if you wash the car for me.*

> *While she was in hospital*, she read three books and wrote ten letters.
> She read three books, *while she was in hospital*, and wrote ten letters.
>   but
> She read three books and wrote ten letters *while she was in hospital.*

In both these examples, the clause beginning with the word *if** or *while** (the *subordinate clause*) has commas surrounding it when it occurs at the beginning or in the middle of the sentence. It does not require commas when it occurs at the end of the sentence.

*If introduces the subordinate clause which is an *adverbial clause of condition*.
*While, a subordinate clause, introduces an *adverbial clause of time* (during the time that).

10. Words such as *although, even though, despite, in spite of, while* and *whereas* can also introduce a contrast. A comma would be used between the two contrasting statements to emphasise the contrast.
Example:

> *Although she was a tall person*, she could not reach the top shelf.
> *Despite having a bad cold*, he played soccer.
> Tim was shy, *whereas his sister was lively and extrovert*.

11. To separate two clauses when the subject of each clause is different.
Example:

> Jane likes to read books, and John likes cycling.

Coordinating Clauses.   For those who need more information.
A *compound* sentence is made up of two or more *co-ordinating clauses.*
Co-ordinating clauses are of equal status and are joined together with a conjunction such as *and*, *but* and *or*.

A comma should precede the conjunction when the subject (the thing we are talking about) changes, especially when by doing so, the sense of what you are writing is enhanced.
Example:

> John held open the door, and Janet entered the room.

However, if the subject of the sentence remains the same, there is usually no comma.
Example:

> Jane likes to read and (she likes to) cycle.
> John opened the door and (John) went inside.

There are times when you must decide when to put in a comma and when it is better to leave one out. If it makes what you are writing easier to read and understand especially in a long complicated sentence, certainly add a comma. However, I would suggest a comma is added to emphasise contrast even when the subject of the sentence remains the same.
Example:

> Jane loves to read, but hates to sew.
> Jacky is highly intelligent, but on this occasion she seemed to go to pieces.
> The train set off on time, but arrived late.

PRACTICE 4 : THE COMMA

A comma is used:

9.   **To separate groups of words beginning with words such as *when,* *after, before, until, if, while* and *although* from the remaining part of the sentence if they come at the beginning or in the middle of the sentence. No comma is needed if they come at the end.**
10. **To emphasise contrast.**
11. **To separate two clauses when the subject of each clause is different.**

Exercise Twenty:_____

Each of the following sentences contains a group of words beginning with words such as *when, after, before, until* and *although*. With reference to Rule 9 above, write out each sentence adding commas where necessary. Some of the sentences may not need commas.

1.   Although it was nightfall he could see the lake clearly.

2.   I'll stay at home if it rains.

3.   Because you were so late getting changed we chose our team without you.

4.   The train was eight minutes late when it arrived.

5.   If he asks me I'll help him.

6.   I can't afford to go on holiday because I haven't any money.

7.   She thought that after she had finished her homework she'd watch television.

8.   Your brother never gets out of the swimming pool until the very last minute.

9.   Sandra thought that although it was expensive she would buy that new dress.

10. Despite his intelligence Matthew still makes silly mistakes.

Exercise Twenty-One:_____

Each of the following sentences contains a group of words beginning with words such as *when, after, before, until* and *although*. With reference to Rule 9 above, write out each sentence adding commas where necessary. Some of the sentences may not need commas.

1.   Until you behave properly you cannot go.

2.   If you have your hair cut you can take me to the cinema.

3. The family decided that when the winter was over they'd go somewhere hot for their holidays.

4. The match will continue if the rain stops.

5. Unless you stop that I shall tell my mum.

6. He realised that even if he did have the money he was too busy to take a week off.

7. I expect you will be good while I'm away.

8. Even though she was plump she still won the beauty competition.

9. I think if you make those few alterations your dress will fit.

10. Harry was quite exhausted when he finished the decorating.

Exercise Twenty-Two: _____

Each of the following sentences contains a group of words beginning with words such as *when, after, before, until* and *although* **or** contains two clauses. With reference to Rules 9 and 11 above, write out each sentence adding commas where necessary. Some of the sentences may not need commas.

1. James loves to play the keyboard but Sara prefers to draw and paint.

2. Unless you stop crying your eyes will still be red when Mark arrives.

3. Jessica has a bath and goes to bed early every night.

4. Kingston Rovers won the last match but drew three-all last Saturday.

5. Why Mrs Thomas came so late no one could understand.

6. Until you learn to behave yourself properly in company you will stay in your room.

7. The decorator has finished but the carpenter still has to hang the doors.

8. Can I go to the cinema if I pay for myself?

9. The essay showed the student had considerable creative ability and imagination.

10. Two is a factor of four and three is a factor of nine.

12. A comma is *usually* used at the end of each line of an address.
Example:

Chestnut Cottage,
Lovely Lane,
Sunnytown.

There is a choice here nowadays. While it remains correct to write a comma at the end of every line of an address except the final line which ends in a full stop, it is also acceptable to miss out the commas completely. Either method of punctuation is acceptable. What is incorrect is to use commas at the end of some lines of an address and to omit them at the end of other lines of the same address.

The name of a city is separated from the name of the county or country using a comma. A comma follows the county or country when other words follow in a sentence.
Example:

> I was born in Hull, Yorkshire, England.
> You were born in London, England, and he was born in Paris, France.

13. In a letter:
> **A comma is used at the beginning, after the initial greeting:**
> > Dear Sue,   Dear Aunt Janet,   Dear Sir,

A comma is used after the final greeting:
> > Yours sincerely,   Yours faithfully,   With love,   Kind regards,

Use *Yours sincerely* (capital *Y*, small *s*) at the end of a formal letter where the initial greeting addresses a person by name.
Use *Yours faithfully* (capital *Y*, small *f*) at the end of a formal letter where the initial greeting begins Dear Sir, or Dear Madam.

14. In the date, a comma is placed between the day of the week, the date and the month, and the year.
Example:

> Tuesday, 15th December, 1981.
> Wednesday, 8th August, 1984.

15. A comma is used in numbers to separate the millions from the thousands and from the hundreds, tens and units.
Example:

> *42,879,105*

Starting on the right and working to the left, put in the comma after every group of three figures. A comma, however, is not put into figures designating the year: 1984, 1995 - these do not require commas.

16. A comma is used before and often after direct speech.
Example:

> "Please," said Sally, "I would like to come too."
> Jack turned sharply and said, "You must be kidding! You couldn't hurt a fly!"

In direct speech, a comma is always used immediately before opening the first set of speech marks.
A comma also takes the place of a full stop at the end of the actual words spoken if the narration continues, as Pattern One will demonstrate in the section on Speech in this

Series of books. (See *Punctuation Rules and Practice 2* for notes and Exercises on *Direct and Reported Speech*.)

PRACTICE 5 : THE COMMA

A comma is used:
    12. Usually at the end of each line of an address.
    13. In a letter after an initial greeting and after the final greeting.
    14. In the date to separate the day of the week, the date and the month, and the year.
    15. In numbers.
    16. Before and often after direct speech. (See *Rules and Practice 2*.)

Exercise Twenty-Three: _____

Write out the words and figures below adding commas where necessary. Set out correctly the addresses remembering to add a full stop at the very end.

Example: Mr Sandell 20 Primrose Way Roberts Wood Ipswich
becomes: Mr Sandell,
                     20, Primrose Way,
                     Roberts Wood,
                     Ipswich.

1.   James was born on Wednesday 8th August 1984.

2.   Sara will be fifteen on the 15th December 1996.

3.   Michael was born in Norwich Norfolk but his sister was born in Penn Buckinghamshire.

4.   Christopher's address is Seasons Charlton Hill Denham Buckinghamshire.

5.   5697834

6.   On Saturday 25th July I am going to San Francisco America.

7.   Dear Sir Please accept my apologies Yours sincerely John Smith.

8.   8563094821

9.   She is coming to stay on 2nd November 1994.

10.   Have you ever been to London England or Paris France?

Listed overleaf, then, are the sixteen different uses of the comma.

SUMMARY : THE COMMA

There are **16** uses of the comma.

We use commas to separate:

1. Items in a list or series in place of the words *and* or *or*.

2. The name or title of a person being addressed.

3. *Yes, no, well, please* and *thank you* when part of a spoken answer.

4. *Question phrases* such as *aren't you?* added to the end of a sentence.

5. Groups of words which are not absolutely necessary to the meaning of
    the sentence. These can:
    a.   begin with *who, which, whose,* or *whom.*
    b.   begin with a word ending in *ed* or *ing.*
    c.   when the group of words is used as description of the main topic.

6. Specific words such as *however, meanwhile, moreover, nevertheless*
    from the rest of the sentence.

7. Other words or groups of words where necessary to avoid ambiguity.

8. Exclamations when they are part of the sentence.

9. Groups of words at the beginning or in the middle of the sentence
    which begin with such words as *when, although, because, unless, if* and
    while.

10. To emphasise contrast.

11. Clauses, when the subject of each clause is different.

12. At the end of each line of an address.

13. In a letter - following the initial and final greetings.

14. In the date to separate the day of the week, the date and the month,
    and the year.

15. In numbers to separate millions from thousands, hundreds tens and
    units.

16. In speech, before the opening speech mark and at the end of the words
    actually spoken if the narration continues. (See *Rules and Practice 2.*)

RULE SUMMARIES

Here you are asked to do three things:

1. Read through all the Rules that have been identified in this book, one at a time.
2. When you are ready, fill in the missing words in the Rule Summaries below.
3. Explain in your own words what is meant by each Rule, making references to the examples given.

THE SENTENCE

Read Pages 2 to 3 about **THE SENTENCE** and when you are ready complete the following Rule Summary without referring to those pages.

A SENTENCE is a _____ of words which:
1. Tries to articulate a _____ and unified idea.
2. Makes _____ _____ by itself, and as such,
3. Can _____ _____.
It needs no other _____ to complete it.

Now turn back to page 3 to check your answer.

KEEPING YOUR OWN RECORD OF THE PUNCTUATION RULES IN THESE BOOKS

To keep a permanent record of the Punctuation Rules in these books - a record to which you can refer at any time - you need a pack of 5ins x 8ins index cards and an index card box or A5 file.

CARD ONE:
Copy the Rule Summary concerning **THE SENTENCE** from page 3 carefully and clearly onto the first side of Card One. Spread out your writing so it is neat and easy to read.

On the reverse of Card One:
1. Explain what is meant by a *simple* and a *complex sentence* (read pages 4 and 5).
2. Explain what is meant by a *main clause*, a *subordinate clause* and what the difference is between them - that one could stand as a sentence in its own right - which one? The other can do the work of an adjective, adverb etc.
3. What is a *compound sentence*? (Read page 6.)
4. What is a *co-ordinating clause* and how are co-ordinating clauses joined together?
5. What is a *phrase*?
In all cases, give as many examples as you feel are necessary to illustrate and clarify your own notes.

CARD TWO:
Read pages 7 to 10 about the **STRUCTURE OF THE SENTENCE** and in particular **CAPITAL LETTERS**. Then, when you are ready, complete the following Rule Summary without reference to those pages.

Every sentence has its structure defined in three terms. It must have:
1. A _____ _____ at the beginning.
2. A final _____ mark at the end. And,
3. A _____ and _____ containing a _____ verb.

CAPITAL LETTERS

Every sentence must begin with a _____ _____.
There are _____ other uses of the capital letter:
1. For the _____ __.
2. For _____ nouns, _____ words and points of the _____ when they
    are part of a _____.
3. For the _____ of the week and the _____ of the year.
4. Describing words formed from _____ _____.
5. The main words of a _____ of a book, play, T.V. programme etc.
6. At the beginning of each line of _____.
7. For each word in an _____.
8. Initials and many _____ are written in capital letters.
9. The first word spoken in _____ speech is always a capital letter.

Turn to pages 7 and 10 to correct your answers. Then copy the above Rules onto the first side of Card Two.

On the reverse of Card Two:
Under separate Rule side-headings, discuss and give examples for each of the ten parts of the Rule.
For example, under the side heading *2. Capital Letters are used for Proper Nouns*, list examples to show
this and make any extra notes about names which consist of more than one word, foreign names, and capital
letters used in a religious and geographic context.
Make your notes as comprehensive as possible so you will be able to refer to them in the future without
looking up again what is *really* meant by the points you are making.

CARD THREE:
Read through the notes on **FINAL PUNCTUATION MARKS** on pages 11 to 14. When you are ready,
complete the following Rule Summaries.

There are _____ punctuation marks that can end a sentence:
1. A ____ _____( )
2. A _____ _____ ( )
3. An _____ _____ ( )

A full stop is used at the end of a _____ and a _____.
A question mark is used at the end of a _____. Use a question mark only at the
end of the words _____ _____.
An exclamation mark is used at the end of a sharp expression of _____, often
_____, _____, _____ or humour. An exclamation is often said loudly,
_____ or stressed.
Always use an excalamtion mark:
1. At the end of a sentence beginning with _____ or _____ which does not ask a
    question.
2. A sharp or sudden exclamation _____ by _____.
3. A _____ called by itself and not as part of a sentence.

A question mark and an exclamation mark take the place of a _____ _____ and
must be followed by a _____ letter.

© *1994 Susan J. Daughtrey M.Ed.*

Read through the notes on page 14, correct your Rule Summary and copy it neatly onto the first side of Card Three.

On the reverse of Card Three answer the following three points:
1. What are the four main types of sentence? Which punctuation mark is used to end each type?
2. What is another name for a question? A command?
3. Discuss in detail the exclamation mark. Make your own notes about when to use an exclamation mark.

CARD FOUR:

Read the notes on pages 16 and 17 concerning **THE FULL STOP USED IN INITIALS AND ABBREVIATIONS** and when you are ready, complete the following Rule Summary without referring to that section.

Initials and Abbreviations are usually followed by a _____ _____ except an abbreviated _____ unit and _____ currency. All other punctuation in the sentence remains the _____.
_____ dots can be used to show the _____ of a word or words.

Turn to page 17, correct this Rule Summary and then carefully copy it onto the first side of Card Four.

On the reverse of Card Four:
1. When are capital letters used in abbreviations? Give examples to show this.
2. Explain what the full stop is doing in abbreviations such as adj., sing., geog.
3. In which abbreviations is the full stop *tending* to be omitted? Give examples.
4. What is an *acronym*? Give examples.
5. When do we *certainly* not use a full stop in an abbreviation? Give examples.
6. Explain in your own words what effect, if any, this abbreviation mark has on the punctuation of the sentence. Give examples.
7. Explain what is meant by, and how, an *omission* is shown.

CARD FIVE:

Read through the notes on pages 18 to 20 about **THE COMMA** and when you are ready, complete the following Rule Summary without referring to those pages.

There are ____ uses of the Comma. The first 4 uses are:
1. Use a comma to separate items in a _____ or _____.
2. In a term of _____, that is, when _____ someone by _____.
3. When _____, _____, _____, _____ and _____ _____ is part of the spoken answer.
4. To separate _____ phrases such as _____ *you?* _____ *you?* which are added to the _____ of the sentence.

Read page 20 and correct your answers. Copy these four rules from page 20 onto the first side of Card Five.

On the reverse of that Card:
1. What does the comma replace in the first Rule above. When is the *and* or *or* kept? What three types of item or action may be *listed* in this way?
2. Under what circumstances might a *listing* be written without commas? (clue: great big dog) Why?
3. When speaking to someone, their name, status or title is separated from the rest of the words in the sentence by a comma or commas. Discuss, giving examples.
4. Give examples to illustrate Rules 3 and 4 above.

CARD SIX and CARD SEVEN:
Read pages 22 to 27 for more uses of **THE COMMA.** When you are ready complete the following Rule Summary without referring to those pages.

A comma or commas is used to separate groups of words from the rest of the sentence. There are _____ groups of words which contain information which is not absolutely necessary to the meaning of the sentence. These are:

1. When the group of words begins with _____, _____, _____, or _____.
2. When the first word of the group ends in _____ or _____.
3. When the group of words is used as _____.

Read page 27 to check your answer. Then copy carefully and clearly the Rule Summary on page 27 on to the first side of Card Six.

On the reverse of Card Six:
1. Copy the first example on page 22 and in your own words discuss why the reader does not need the words *who likes to ride his bike to school* to fully understand *who* Nicholas is. Explain that we already know, and that this clause is simply giving us *more information about Nicholas*. Use other examples, either from the book or of your own, to fully explain this. If you wish, refer to the proper name of these clauses and explain what is meant by a *non-restrictive relative clause*.

On the first side of Card Seven:
2. Copy the example given on page 24, *A car that stalls is of little use*. Discuss why it is necessary to keep the group of words beginning with *that* in order for the reader to understand what the author is saying - that without these words, the sentence is incomplete - that these words are necessary for the reader to understand *which car* the author is writing about. Give more examples, including examples of your own, to illustrate the point you are making. If you refer to the notes under the title *For those who need to know more*, talk about *restrictive relative clauses* and what they are and what they do.

On the reverse of Card Seven:
3. Read page 26 and explain in your own words Rule B. If it is helpful, make reference to a *participle clause* and explain how it gets its name,
4. Read Rule C on page 27 and explain that these descriptions, which are often no more that the subject's name, are usually found next to the person or thing they are describing. Give examples to illustrate this.

CARD EIGHT:
Read pages 30 and 31 on three more uses of **THE COMMA** and when you are ready, complete the following Rule Summary without referring to those pages.

1. Specific words such as _____ and _____ are separated from the rest of the sentence by a comma.
2. Other words may be separated to avoid _____
3. _____, when they are part of a sentence, are also separated from the rest of the sentence by a comma.

Read page 31 and check you answers. When you are ready, copy this Rule Summary neatly and clearly onto the first side of Card Eight.

On the reverse of Card Eight:
1. Explain in detail these three uses of the comma. Give examples of your own as well as from the text, to illustrate your answer.
2. Be sure you understand what is meant by *ambiguity*.
3. Can you think of any humorous or interesting sentences where without the comma the ambiguity would also be amusing?

CARD NINE:

Read pages 32 and 33 for two more uses of **THE COMMA**. When you are ready complete the following Rule Summary without referring to those pages.

A comma is used:
1. To separate groups of words beginning with words such as _____, _____, _____, _____, ____, _____ and _____ from the remaining part of the sentence if they come at the beginning or in the middle of the sentence.
2. To emphasise _____.
3. To separate two _____ when the _____ of each clause is different.

Check your answer by referring to page 34, then copy these Rule Summaries onto the first side of Card Nine.

On the reverse of Card Nine:
1. Explain in your own words a *complex sentence*, a *main* and *subordinate clause*.
2. Explain why a comma or commas is used only when groups of words beginning with *while*, *although* *before* etc. come at the beginning or in the middle of a sentence, and not when they occur at the end of a sentence.
3. Give examples to show the use of a comma in contrasting statements.
4. Discuss the use of a comma to separate two clauses which have different subjects. Give examples. Contrast this with a sentence which has two clauses but only one subject.

CARD TEN:

Read pages 36 to 37 for five further uses of **THE COMMA**. When you are ready, complete the following Rule Summary with referring to those pages.

A comma is used:
1. Usually at the ____ of each line of an _____.
2. In a _____ after an _____ greeting and after the _____ greeting.
3. In the _____ to separate the day of the _____, the_____ and the month, and the _____.
4. In _____.
5. Before and after _____ speech.

Check your answers by referring to page 37 and then copy carefully these final five uses of **THE COMMA** onto the first side of Card Ten.

On the reverse make any notes from pages 36 and 37, with examples, which you feel are of importance to you. For example, note that the name or a town or county is separated from the name of a country with a comma. Record which final greeting to use at the bottom of business and formal letters.

A N S W E R S

Exercise 1

2. The sun shone brightly.
5. She went shopping.
7. Do your homework.
8. That exercise is silly.
10. I like to travel by car.

Exercise 2

2. I have a kitten called Harry.
3. Draw the curtains.
5. He opened his eyes.
8. John will have a piece of chocolate.
9. You need a new pair of shoes.

Exercise 3

2. I like swimming.
5. It is Jessica's birthday.
6. You can have a new pair of trainers.
7. I can help.
8. The tyre is flat.

Exercise 4

1. It was raining. Michael decided to take his umbrella.
2. Sandra was tired so she decided to go to bed early.
3. Come to my house to watch television.
4. I like school best on Saturday.
5. My shoes need repairing. They let in water.
6. In my bag there's a pen.
7. We can go to the beach. Take a towel.
8. The football pitch was muddy. We slipped about.
9. The radio is too loud. Please turn it down.
10. The roses are beautiful. They have lasted a long time.

Exercise 5

1. It's raining. I must go or I shall get wet.
2. The phone rang just as I was about to leave.
3. In her bag there's a book. Take it to her. She needs it now.
4. The dog needs taking for a walk. He's gone to get his lead.
5. The newspaper boy is late. He was late yesterday and the day before.
6. Let's go shopping. I need to buy a new pair of shoes.
7. This will have to wait. I'm busy making tea. I haven't got the time.
8. After I've done my homework, I'm going to watch T.V.
9. I like to play badminton. I'm in the county team now.
10. Sara wears a funny hat. She's got orange hair as well.
11. Christopher has an American tea shirt on. It looks swell.

Exercise 6

1. The French President is visiting London next September.
2. Nicholas and Jason go to Fairfield Middle School.
3. I went to see the film 'Denis' at the Tower Cinema last Thursday.
4. Michael is going to Paris, France, on a school trip in July.
5. Gemma's Aunt Janet is visiting her in Norwich, this summer.
6. M.P. stands for Member of Parliament, P.M. for Prime
7. Brian wants to drive his Porsche to Germany.

8. James and I went to visit Windsor Castle to see the Queen.
9. Sara has read 'The Animals of Farthing Wood' and 'The Wind in the Willows'.
10. I went with Bernard to see Barry at Kingston General Hospital.

Exercise 7

1. What time is it? It's time you went to bed.
2. He asked what time it was. Why does he need to know?
3. Jenny asked how much the dress cost.
4. Nicky asked the little girl if she was lost.
5. Where can I get an interesting book?
6. James wondered what time Khaled would come.
7. Dale and Liam want to know what they're having for tea.
8. What is the capital of Egypt?
9. Don't you ask a lot of questions.
10. Can't you close the back door behind you?

Exercise 8

1. What a hot day! Do you want to swim? I think it would be glorious.
2. Gosh! Have you seen her hair! It's bright purple! I think she's overdone it this time.
3. How silly! You've got your clothes wet. How did you do that?
4. Sam! Stop! What an idiot you are! You've just backed into that Mercedes.
5. I have to ask if you can drive. It strikes me you still need lessons!
6. What time is it? I'm supposed to be at Samantha's house by seven o'clock.
7. What a clumsy girl you are! Didn't you see the ink? Now it's all over the carpet.
8. Did you ask if you were in the team this week? He said you should ask him.
9. Thank goodness, it's Friday! I can stay in bed in the morning.
10. Are you going camping this summer? We need to ask if we can come.

Exercise 9

1. Roald Dahl wrote the 'B.F.G.', 'Witches', 'Boy'... I've forgotten the others.
2. The M.P. for Hull is Barry Brocklehurst.
3. There are ten mm in one cm.
4. In the dictionary it said happiness n., happy adj. I know what that means.
5. August (Aug.) and September (Sept.) are the eighth and ninth months of the year.
6. There are 100p in £1.
7. Put the T.V. on. There's a good programme on the B.B.C.
8. Knives, forks, spoons etc. are called cutlery.
9. Hot countries, e.g. Africa, are often dry.
10. The plural (pl.) of knife (sing.) is knives.

Exercise 10

1. Sandra ate an apple, an orange and a whole grapefruit this evening.

Exercise 10 contd.

2. Lee has worked in a newsagent, a hospital and a garage as part of his 'Work Experience'.
3. Anderson, Hardy and Owen must report to Mr. Jones immediately.
4. A big furry cat with long white whiskers has just walked across the lawn.
5. He kicked the ball hard, low and fast, straight into the hands of the waiting goal-keeper.
6. Ice-skating, swimming and dancing are my favourite pastimes.
7. Please tidy your room, make your bed and walk the dog before you go to bed.
8. The old man had a brown, well-weathered and wrinkled face.
9. A pilot must learn to climb, bank, roll and stall his plane.
10. Pick up the bucket and spade, the wet swimming clothes, the picnic basket and the newspaper.

Exercise 11

1. Please, Miss, I need to go to the cloakroom.
2. Stuart, pass me that book.
3. Will you, Caroline, show Miss Jones where to go?
4. I say, Miss Hardy, that's a pretty dress you are wearing.
5. When do I take the medicine, Dr Cooper?
6. Fido, stop chasing the cat!
7. Michael, go to bed at once!
8. I haven't got a pencil, sir.
9. Alice and Fred want to go too, Mary.
10. Take Nicholas to Mr. Smith's room at once, Jonathan.

Exercise 12

1. Pick up your bicycle, James, and put it in the shed next to the lawnmower, secateurs and garden shears.
2. I beg your pardon, sir, but I left the books, pens, pencils and rulers on your desk.
3. Tonight, my friends, is a special occasion. It is the shared birthday party of Susan, Maureen and Hilary. Happy birthday, girls!
4. Sir, the French teacher has asked Barry and I to go to the staffroom to carry some books. May we be excused?
5. My sister has had measles, mumps and chicken pox and she's only eight!
6. Good evening, ladies and gentlemen. In front of you there should be paper, a pencil and a pen. Shall we proceed with the first item on the agenda?
7. Gosh, Sam! What have you got? You were asked to get two tins of beans, a packet of biscuits and a loaf of bread.
8. The hardest working, most diligent and keenest person I know, Sam, is you.
9. I wonder what Jo is doing. Do you think he is alright, Sue?
10. Stop! Stop, exactly where you are! What are you boys doing? Speak, boy, speak! I'm asking you a question!

Exercise 13

1. Sara, have you seen the film 'Jurassic Park'? My brother was a bit frightened by the dinosaurs, weren't you, David?
2. Well, I never! You've eaten up all your cabbage. You said you didn't like cabbage, didn't you?
3. Sally made the sandwiches, packed the cool box, put it in the car and set off in great excitement. She spent most of the day in a traffic jam!
4. Follow me, men. We need to hide. Go around that tree, through the hedge, over the stile and down the bank. They'll never see us there.
5. Operator, I've been cut off. Can you help me? I was talking to my aunt when the line went dead. Oh, thank you, that's better!
6. You can manage that big bag of shopping, can't you? Well, thank you, young man. That's very kind of you.

Exercise 14

1. I would like you all to make Mrs Williams, who is coming to speak to us this afternoon, very welcome.(X)
2. James Bowey, who owns a new mountain bike, is in my class.(X)
3. The car that broke down is being towed to the garage. (√)
4. I went to fill the car which had run out of petrol. (√)
5. Mary, who had the clearest voice, was given the leading role in the play. (X)
6. Blenheim Palace, which the class visited last summer, is near Oxford. (X)
7. A boy who has a hobby will not be bored. (√)
8. My brother Mark, who is in the army, is coming home for Christmas. (X)
9. A pen that won't write is of little use. (√)
10. Sally, whose brother is a pop singer, is my best friend. (X)

Exercise 15

1. Will the boy who threw that piece of chalk please own up. (√)
2. We go to Norfolk, which is a lovely part of the country, for our holidays. (X)
3. Jane collected the suit which had been taken for drycleaning. (√)
4. The china plate which already had a crack in it broke when I dropped it. (√)
5. The village store, which sells everything from crisps to crockery, is run by Mrs Bailey. (X)
6. Is there anybody here who can hear me? (√)
7. I have not yet seen Dr. Davis, who is our new form teacher. (X)
8. Will the person who parked a red sports car in front of the gates remove it at once? (√)
9. This is the road that goes to town. (√)
10. A student who works hard for his examinations will do well.(√)

Exercise 16

1. Trying to be helpful, Brenda only made things worse.
2. Blowing up the balloon, Simon looked like a fat-cheeked little elf.
3. Peter, sobbing uncontrollably, could hardly speak.
4. Tired of her independence, Carol came home.
5. Stumbling along the path, the tired and hungry scouts were looking for shelter.
6. Mr. Harding, losing his temper, shouted at the class.
7. Maureen set off for her first dance dressed in her prettiest dress.
8. Feeling rather ill, he stumbled to the telephone.

Exercise 16 contd.

9. The apples, falling off the tree, were collected by the children below.
10. Chuckling quietly to himself, David left the room.

Exercise 17

1. Shaun, my nephew, is an excellent driver.
2. The class was surprised when Michael Higgins, a disruptive student, was made a prefect.
3. Mrs. Kaye, our neighbour, kindly offered to look after the kittens while we were on holiday.
4. 'Spindrift', the largest boat in the harbour, was damaged in the storm.
5. Liam, a tall boy for his age, began school today.
6. His car, a blue sports car, travels fast.
7. Vesuvius, the famous volcano, is in Italy.
8. The headmaster introduced Mr. Hicks, the guest speaker.
9. My neices, Jessica and Jade, are going with us.
10. They spent their holidays in Gstaad, a mountain resort.

Exercise 18

1. The girl who lives next door is in my class.
2. Leaving early, he beat the traffic.
3. The ice-cream which we bought was so soft it melted before we could eat it.
4. Thinking quickly, Jeanne delivered the argument that won the debate for her team.
5. Tom Carpenter, form captain, took the assembly today.
6. The train which was empty was on its way to London.
7. Dressed smartly in his new suit, he left for the interview.
8. The bird with the worm arrived early.
9. Mr Higgins, our form teacher, likes reading books.
10. Arthur, the football coach, worked hard for the team.

Exercise 19

1. It was, without doubt, the worst restaurant I had ever been in.
2. I wonder, by the way, if you could tell me the way to the city centre?
3. She agreed to go, however. (or no comma)
4. Naturally, I would love to go.
5. Oh, I say, that looks super!
6. He was, nevertheless, determined to go. (or no commas)
7. We shall meet again, no doubt.
8. It is, therefore, my privilege to open this new library.
9. Well, I must be going now.
10. By the way, do you remember her?

Exercise 20

1. Although it was nightfall, he could see the lake clearly.
2. I'll stay at home if it rains.
3. Because you were so late getting changed, we chose our team without you.
4. The train was eight minutes late when it arrived.
5. If he asks me, I'll help him.
6. I can't afford to go on holiday because I haven't any money.
7. She thought that, after she had finished her homework, she'd watch television.

8. Your brother never gets out of the swimming pool until the very last minute.
9. Sandra thought that, although it was expensive, she would buy that new dress.
10. Despite his intelligence, Matthew still makes silly mistakes.

Exercise 21

1. Until you behave properly, you cannot go.
2. If you have your hair cut, you can take me to the cinema.
3. The family decided that, when the winter was over, they'd go somewhere hot for their holidays.
4. The match will continue if the rain stops.
5. Unless you stop that, I shall tell my mum.
6. He realised that, even if he did have the money, he was too busy to take the week off work.
7. I expect you will be good while I'm away.
8. Even though she was plump, she still won the beauty competition.
9. I think, if you make those few alterations, your dress will fit.
10. Harry was quite exhausted when he finished the decorating.

Exercise 22

1. James loves to play the keyboard, but Sara prefers to draw and paint.
2. Unless you stop crying, your eyes will still be red when Mark arrives.
3. Jessica has a bath and goes to bed early every night.
4. Kingston Rovers won the last match but drew three-all last Saturday.
5. Why Mrs Thomas came so late, no one could understand.
6. Until you learn to behave yourself properly in company, you will stay in your room.
7. The decorator has finished, but the carpenter still has to hang the doors.
8. Can I go to the cinema if I pay for myself?
9. The essay showed the student had considerable creative ability and imagination.
10. Two is a factor of four, and three is a factor of nine.

Exercise 23

1. James was born on Wednesday, 8th August, 1984.
2. Sara will be fifteen on the 15th December, 1996.
3. Michael was born in Norwich, Norfolk, but his sister was born in Penn, Buckinghamshire.
4. Christopher's address is: Seasons,
   Charlton Hill,
   Denham,
   Buckinghamshire.
5. 5,697,834
6. On Saturday, 25th July, I am going to San Francisco, America.
7. Dear Sir,
   Please accept my apologies.
   Yours sincerely,
   John Smith.
8. 8,563,094,821
9. She is coming to stay on 2nd November, 1994.
10. Have you ever been to London, England, or Paris, France?